Late To A Meeting
A Collection of prose and poetry by
members of The University of East Anglia's
Creative Writing Society

Anthology 2022

Late To A Meeting
First published by Egg Box Publishing 2022

Part of UEA Publishing Project, Ltd.
International ©2022 retained by individual authors
A CIP record for this book is available at the British Library

This book is sold subject to the condition that it shall not, by way of trade or otherwise, be lent, resold, hired out, stored in a retrieval system, or otherwise circulated without the publisher's prior consent in any form of binding or cover other than that in which it is published and without a similar condition including this condition being imposed on the subsequent purchaser.
Late To A Meeting is typeset in Baskerville Regular
Titles are set in Baskerville Bold
Designed and typeset by Mackenzie Malcolm
Printed and bound in the UK by Imprint Digital
Distributed by Inpress
ISBN 978-1-913861-70-4

The Editorial Team

EDITOR-IN-CHIEF — Clara Ehlers

EDITORIAL BOARD — Silas Hand
Barnaby Hill
Samuel Glyn
Ellen Newall
Evan Denison
Emma McDonald
Badriya Abdullah
Katherine Torres Cruz
Sam Kirk
Emma Fawkes
Melissa Garrett
Alec Goldstone
Rosie Kirin-White
Elizabeth Yew
Edward Grierson

COLLABORATORS — Biff Pearson

COVER DESIGN — Becca Blake

TYPESETTING — Mackenzie Malcolm

CONTENTS

Poetry

Reifer	Alex Curry	11
Humans Becoming Things	Allison Ko	12
Cold	Alice Avery	13
Honey		14
Shades of Blue	Alice Cunningham	15
If I Could Hit The Notes Like Ed	Balazs Kokenyesy	16
My Intimate Stranger	Barnaby Hill	18
I Am Not Ozymandias	Biff Pearson	20
My Alter Ego's a Poster Child	Clara Ehlers	22
Half-Full		23
Costa Jon	Clem Hailes	24
Roulette Planète	Eyed Ears	26
You Found Yourself in a Junkyard	Elsy Leslie	28
Mother Nature	Freya Calcluth	30
Godless	Grace Phillips	31
Younge Stranger		32
The Pink Where The Sky Meets The Trees	Hatty Hardy	34
Recipe for Disaster	Helena Keys	35
Melancholy Things	Kyleigh Taylor	36
End Notes	Linda Collins	37
The Garden of Regret	Liz Yew	40
My Soulmate	Max Wrigley	41
Garden of Regret		42
Come Find Me, Lying in the Stream	Sammy Glyn	43
Psalm for the Drowning Sinner	Silas Hand	44
Judical Review into Floodplain Managment		45
Growing Pains	Tallulah Cox	46

Poetry (Content Warning)

Whatever Together	*Ellen Newall* 51
Shh- Listen!	*Brandon Choo* 52
Opening	*E M Fawkes* 54
Self-Talk	*Esther Cornforth* 56
Locked Doors	*Eve Attwood* 57
Thorns	*Helena Keys* 58
Thinking and Other Bad Habits	*Lily Gooch* 59
The Dog is Dead	*Maya Elphick* 61
Tat for Tit	*Sarah Crowe* 62

Prose

A Disturbance	*Edward Grierson* 67
An Inconvenient Affair	*Hannah Rice-Smyth* 69
HARPER	*Harper Day Pope* 70
Albion	*Melissa Garrett* 72
Gold Stars	*Mia Galanti* 74
Morning, The Bathroom, Home	*Molly Phillips* 77
His Green Heart	*Oli Hurley* 80
The Merman	*Sam Kirk* 82

Prose (Content warning)

Before	*Eleanor Lewis* 89
Lifeblood	*Evan Denison* 91
Juliet	*Ingrid Jensen* 95
Oblivion	*Temi Taiwo-Oni* 99
Defy the Devil	*William Mckinnel* 101

Introduction

This year has been exceptionally unexceptional. First years are the guinea pigs for a new way of teaching, and third years are facing the fear of the real world, all while the world is still recovering from Covid. With new combined, remote, in person, online, teaching, teams, zoom, blackboard, ...
It's no wonder that we were Late for a Meeting at one point or another.

Ignore the stress of life on your shoulders and sit back, relax, and read *Late to a Meeting*, including a mix of poetry and prose from members of Creative Writing Society 2021-2022.

Poetry

Reifer

I
trap
rats
name now one man I
a
devil
dewed
draw
never odd or even as a
dessert's
spit
live on reviled

I
part
stars
name now one man
I
a
lived
dewed

ward
never odd or even
as a
stressed
tips
deliver no evil
Alex Curry

humans becoming things
{in 3 progressions}

-

she's seeping through like earl grey tea
the cold milk poured too quickly
spillage occurs
and the translucent white gradually
swirls
darkens
richens
a faint tone of bitterness.

--

dehydrated passion on dehydrated
skin, leathery
my fingers seize up
like a body too long in the sea
as they did to you
wrinkling; unsure;
in a last attempt to cling on − please

[water us]

---

laterally i lay and the world becomes tilted
i gasp,
airflow sideways and trickles of my dinner crouch and wiggle
through the crawlspace that is the esophagus.

Allison Ko

Cold

Whispers,
shared between our eyes,
evening light.
The night seeps through
the locked catch, leaving frost
on the sill like breath.

Ice on your tongue,
slippery, and I've been crashing
into your molars, lodging myself
into your gums.
Emergency lights blink
on the ridged roof of your mouth.

Heated blanket on the bed,
weighted, keeping you there
'till morning.

I'm worried the warmth
will melt the snow
entrenched in your nails.

Will the water be salty or fresh
when I press my tongue
to these damp spots you've left?

Alice Avery

Honey

Gold,
like Icarus'
flightless feathers
fall. Sticky droplets of
sweet wine drizzled by skilled
hands into goblets warmed by the sun
Helios dancing on the blinding glint as they
roll over softened bones. Then savour rich oil on
stretched canvases, white knuckles in silk sheets. Nectar
from Nectarine, pearled, dripping from curved shell ribs, nacre
coated skin, Venus' footprint on the sea, salt stroking at the heel
to stay close to soft unused creases. Caught in the sunlight as it
drips off the chin, suspended, like starlight, the shared breath of
a kiss. Fall tears tasting of gold.

Alice Avery

Shades of Blue

You start at my eyes, softly tracing the purpled lids,
your thumb fanning out my lashes. Then,
my rounded cheeks, bruised with rouge,
an index finger orbiting the plush flesh, down
to my chin, smudging the wine-red drops across my lips;
too dark to be just paint.
Outlining my neck until
you reach the jutting edge of my collarbone,
dappling indigo across the vast expanse of skin.
Brushes of lavender accentuate the weighted flesh of my breast,
the tender warmth easiest to stain with your unpredictable
shades of blue.
Swelling my gentle canvas with Aegean, mulberry, mauve and
admiral until there is no space free from the ache.
I was taught to believe that art can be found in even the darkest
places,
and that all of it is beautiful.
Even when it hurts.

Alice Cunningham

If I Could Hit The Notes Like Ed

I used to wish night and day to hit the notes like Ed
Craved it like a predator craves its precious prey's meat
'Cause I once believed I had the talent
to sing softly and soulfully like a heavenly angel.
Then puberty hit, and everything went to shit
Nothing worked, I was changing for the worse.
Sometimes, when I unnecessarily tortured myself
by trying to sing along to songs I couldn't sing
I thought I couldn't sing at all anymore.

Ed was who I wished to be
The lyrics and the voice;
There was also Nate
who used to belt out tenor notes.
I used to believe that they were the right thing,
They were the ones sought after
They were the ones that sold, the ones who got famous
They were the ones that mattered
The higher the voice the better

'Cause who cares about a low range baritone,
whose weak vocal cords vibrate faintly?
Where were the roles where I'd impress people,
on stage or in front of the camera?
Where was my chance to prove my worth?

All I wished for was for someone to understand me
For someone that feels my pain and with heart try to convince
me why I was wrong
Now, I look back on those days with regret
An angry, lost, and confused soul, wailing for nothing
'Cause I was convinced that I was the great one, whose talent
was taken away
I was like a spoiled child crying over something forbidden

I became what I never wanted
Spoiled, lost, and destructive - just plain bad
How I behaved towards others was inexcusable
I wouldn't listen, even to my parents' kindness.
To everyone who I hurt, I'm deeply sorry.

Now, the situation is much brighter -
I may not be able to sing the stars of the sky
But I know every time I get the chance, I light up the stage
I like the songs that are in my range
I even hit the notes like Ed sometimes
I learned what jealousy can do to someone
And what being selfish turns you into.

Balazs Kokenyesy

My Intimate Stranger

I regard him from my table. His appearance steps into real-time by the bell clinging to the wooden perimeter of the door. My cup of black coffee is a mirror below me. I watch myself.

He deftly plucks the cloth from his face,
To order some combination
Of espresso, hot; sugar; milk, whipped.
He is ten years older, wearing glasses now.
                    Unapologetically,
He finally looks like himself,
                    Uncompelled,
By the sensuality of the negative space in his mind; so as to
Not feel alone.
          And he can't see me, but he still takes me home.
          He undresses his chest,
             Cups my breast as though fondling a memory,
             Pinches it and brings tears to both our eyes.
Unknown art covers his wall,
A haven of glossily finished bright gasps of colour
To muted sighs, speaking as loudly as the silence,
That he used to be.
I see myself, lavishly open, in ink,
A lens to look through
To scrutinise, how much of a man I am,
A hand flourished across our sex,
To sign the name we fought years to wear.

I make love to myself in ten years,
Lost into manifestations and reveries
Lost into masturbatory philosophies,
Lusting after a version of myself
Who writes himself into a man, into existence,
Touching my identity,
Massaging my ego,

Swirling myself into place,
Eyes rolling, pleasantly tiring. Desiring for time to tell,

He taps his fingers to the side of the coffee cup, empty,
Looking to be refilled, fulfilled, until he disintegrates.
And I indulge this empty space, by the espresso-stained countertop,
With the image of the man I am to be.

Barnaby Hill

I am Not Ozymandias

(Although in This Moment I Wish I Was)
I am standing in front of a painting
In an art gallery in Manchester
And all I hear is shuffling footsteps
Across the well traveled floors;
The occasional mutter about a painting
I'm not looking at right now.
Time is moving like sticky honey,
As it tends to when you're pushing
Through it purposefully.
Only choosing to avalanche
When you're some idiot
trying to outlast it.
I continue onto the next painting,
Intending to look at it,
I stand there for a minute or so
Before I realize I'm not looking,
Just standing.
So I move onto the next
And I have to stand behind someone
Who is already staring
At a silver fish on a blue plate
That the artist painted
Out of focus and all the edges blend
Into each other—
Or it could be that I need new glasses.
So I traipse onwards to another,
Except this is a video piece
With images flickering into each other,
All becoming one,
As my shoes start
To melt into the floor
And I decide that it's been
Long enough and I can check my phone again

To see if you've messaged since
Five paintings ago.
And you have.
But it's to tell me that you'll be
Another half an hour late.

Biff Pearson

my alter ego is a poster child

She's learning Mandarin, meanwhile,
I'm pandering to my year eight
English teacher's great expectations.

She's read all of Dickens, meanwhile,
I'm chickening out of holding your hand.
You must understand,

she's done all my homework, meanwhile
I'm stumbling homeward, and hurling
insults at perfect Miss Jekyll,

doctoral candidate.
She might be the devil, meanwhile,
I'm adequate.

Tell me, darling, will you still want me
when I stop injecting serum
concocted from secreted secrets?

(whispers): ego te absolvo

Clara Ehlers

half-full

you look at me and think I'm

empty

except for thoughts of lipgloss
and the odd bubblegum flavoured flutter-fly,
pollinating parrot tulips growing in ashtrays

e m pt y

except for rhinestoned cobwebs,
adorning each cerebral antechamber,
the chamberlain dressed as a playboy bunny,
planning the guillotine castration

EMPTY

except for my mind's heart-shaped pool
in which I lounge on a bright pink float,
a chalice suspended in dainty fingers;
liquid ambiguously oscillating fuckboy excretions
spilling on tan-lined décolletage,
pearl-necklace intact–

oh daddy, still waters run deep.

(all the better to drown you in, dear.)

Clara Ehlers

Costa Jon

Costa Jon is a rather lovely young man
He'll bring you coffee in the morning
Sometimes some bran
Apron tied tight
Embroidered letters bright
As his smile

Starbucks is alright
If you like tax evasion
(and being white)
But have you ever
Been Star-FUCKED
By a Costa boy?
Oh boy oh boy
Full-fat milk (no soy)

That's Costa Jon
Making you cappuccinos
In his burgundy thong
The nation's favourite coffee thot
Costa Jon has a soft spot
In every coffee lovers' heart

But, we have something sacred,
You see?
Costa Jon rarely makes cups of tea
Yet every morning by my bed
Sitting to soothe the hurt in my head -
A cup of loose leaf tea
With a note, just for me:

Off to work,
Hope you have lots of fon*

All my love,
Costa Jon :-)

(*he's northern)

                                                               Clem Hailes

Roulette Planète

Extravagant carpet greets naive feet
As a wondrous gaze marvels all ways,
Laying lingering eyesight upon the flashing machine lights
Arranged around the aisle. Crevices are consumed and defiled,
Invaded by garish neon that enslaves from beyond
The slightly more suave decor
It contrasts with, an effect the refined colour scheme cast
Across the vast neighbouring estate of tables fails to negate.

Wait, that was at 8 this morning - by now the sun is dawning.
Something's wrong, surely you can't have been here that long?
You came in an inexperienced underling, a newbie, you didn't know a thing,
But you came along still, for the same thrill
Everyone gets placing their bets for profits or debts.
Since walking in through that door, it's like you can't even remember anything from before,
You simply sat down in a chair without another care
And whatever ensued after kept your legs glued right there.
In fact, you're still firmly planted in your seat, at the game you take for granted;
No time for fretting about mistakes when you're betting at high stakes.

But you won't be dealt another round of cards - your straying eyes have found
A new game to evoke the same gush of excitement, a familiar rush of adrenaline in your veins.
The entrancing spin of the wheel sends reds and blacks dancing,
Your brain being teased insane by the enticing prospect of gain.
You're already sold - without being told,
Your legs are marching you over, the temptation of wealth luring you in closer.

The chips are down, you hope for the best as your fate rests
On luck; now is your chance to make big bucks.
The dealer looks on with dry eyes, smile propped up atop suit and tie
As the lustrous pearl ball dissipates into the gluttonous whirlpool.
The hypnotic circling sends your own eyes hurtling
In mimicry around their sockets, as you forebode ransacking empty pockets.

Your mother once said you have a knack for keeping track
Of time, but that was back when you still saw the sunshine.
Here, the days - or weeks, or months, or maybe even years -
Pass by slyly, all the while child's play grows dry and grey.

The cycle repeats - the ball is spun, it lands, either you've lost or won,
But still you persist with bet after bet, you can't resist
Fulfilling - if you can call it that - the cravings of the aristocrat.
Gone are the illusions of choice and control, your life and soul
Confined to the table you pray will make you stable.
You've fallen prey to the constructed mould - with each passing day a blip, they
Increase their hold as you fold to the numbers of the black hole.
In all your greed you chase the high, you bleed to feed, until you die.

Then again, who am I to condemn you for being a debtor? I'm no better.

Eyed Ears

"You Found Yourself in a Junkyard"

Do you see how well I've remade myself?
How fine-tuned my authenticity?
I spent my adolescence digging through marbles
For eyes that would look like eyes. You'll find them
Unimpeachable, I reckon, like these lips
I ripped from a tabloid ad, quite a task
When your hands are this little and always in fists.
Okay, ignore the hands. They were a baby doll's.
The arms were a mannequin's and the torso,
A CPR training dummy's—
Disproportionate, maybe, but how masterfully welded at the
Joints! Crazy glue and stage make-up,
Believe it or not. I know, but can
You see the seams? Go on. Look.

Look with the cracks of your goggles, down the broken-button-snub of your nose.
Pick me apart with the prongs where your arms split into fingers.
Gnaw my heart out with the hollow where you should've put a mouth.
You let me know if I bleed.

It seems you found yourself—and forgive me if I'm off base—
In a junkyard, from a skip,
At a binbag split by the weight of itself.
Far be it from me to judge, of course,
But surely you didn't think that patchwork throw would pass for skin?

Now even you will have noticed this untenable stiffness
And I admit this gets less convincing the more I strain around the fixtures, so no,
I don't tend to move this much around anyone who still has their flesh,

And even as I speak I'm battling the notion that I might revert
If only I would surrender this
Cruelty.

Yeah perhaps. But none of us, not even you or I
Are so vain we would shoulder bruises just
For the novelty, the glamour
Of being flush and plump and bruisable.

Elsy Leslie

Mother Nature

When I die, I wish for no fantasticals,
No ceremonies and no mourners;
Humanity should not touch the nature of death,
The beautiful loneliness of our end.

I wish to be buried in the forest.
I want Mother to devour me into Her dirt,
Her tears to fall on my withering corpse,
Her words to call me into her blessings.

Mother Earth has gifted life to corrupted evil;
In turn, my pollution will wither into nutrients
For Her to grow my brothers and sisters,
Her children She never got to meet.

I wish them to cure our cursed faults—
Or for them to return swiftly to the lakes,
And the mountains and the gardens,
As She tries again to create beings
In an image as pure as her.

Freya Calcluth

Godless

The sun-storm races through. It bleaches me with light, makes
me blotched and obvious; the scrapings of old stardust.

I want to be eternal
like the God that I was taught — cross-legged in the hall,
and her rings would rattle as she spoke; palm-against-palm, the
docile sermon,
with faith sold as fact
until my dad told me
it was wolves who lapped up the man from the tomb.

All at once
I was the center.
I was made so small,
passed, as an atom, through space lingering for a breath
that fades from the lips.

The sun-storm races through, and lifts me to the hills.

My outstretched hand
eclipses the sun
and still, I am small.

I see the horizon,
running away, like melted time.

The ocean bounces light,
never still for a moment,
and stretching far, far, far out of sight

and with the great sun-storm I will be gone,

absolved of my words
with the coming of dawn.

Grace Phillips

Young Stranger

Absorbed in the world of an angel (or a fairy, a dove),
I find myself trying to uncover you.

Your odds and ends are scattered- I see you, mostly, in stories.

Flickers of digital light,
scraped-up blurs made timeless, ghosting in my periphery.

But also your own stories.
The bottled-up worlds
that enthral you for weeks on end.

Thought-riddled
little one, with your jaw set
soft and even. Sun-spotted clouds. Unfurled white ribbons
that trace and tickle
the edges of your skull.

Baby of light
and wriggling.
Blonde-white curls and buck teeth, a hum caught, always,
on your breath.

I watch you as a stranger.

I can't find the words
to place in your mouth, or tuck behind your ear. We seem splintered, somehow. Undone.
I am not who you picture.

The words that lick
the inside of your skull
contain no glimpse of me.
I guess you're no psychic.

You fidget within the cage of yourself. That, at least, has remained,
but it's a different breed of restless. It catches on the heart,

little hooks, little half-moon curls of sword edges.

The angel spoke,
about the flat-ridged fringe of the earth.

And it's that
that lingers, in the end.

Grace Phillips

The Pink where the Sky meets the Trees

I wonder if all the world's gentleness comes From the pink where the sky meets the trees. An endless horizon of lingering sun, Underneath the soft gloaming breeze.

This colour is in my sister's cheeks,
And in my best friend's laugh,
The apricot tint of a longed-for hug,
An unseen photograph.

So if I ever need the chance,
To find a moment of peace,
I'll go to where the swallows dance,
At the pink where the sky meets the trees.

Hatty Hardy

Recipe for Disaster

Step 1: Sift sleepless nights into a large bowl until thoroughly tired.

Step 2: Add overdue energy bill and combine until the mixture is completely stressed.

Step 3: Into a saucepan, combine empty cupboards and dirty laundry and let simmer on a medium heat. As soon as bubbles of despair pop from the mix, ramp up to high heat.

Step 4: Drip in motorway traffic and decaf coffee. Continuously stir until foamed rage spills from the saucepan.

Step 5: Incorporate the large bowl of sleepless nights and overdue energy bills until the mixture turns an ominous black.

Step 6: Now, add a pinch of unresponsive landlord. The mixture should be screaming violently if made correctly.

Step 7: Place the saucepan into the microwave and cook on high for 20 minutes. Your mixture is done when completely given up.

<u>Serving suggestion:</u> 1 bottle of high percentage vodka.

Helena Keys

melancholy things

the first morning breath and the taste of celery rice,
my childhood home on my tongue. adult games
on thirteen-year-old phones, naïve and
ignorant of their true meaning. drunk boys
who are nice when they're sober and the shade
of eyeshadow she wore to prom, flush red
as her laugh. kissing the velvet head of my dog
one last time and saying goodbye
to all my friends from high school (don't forget us, okay?).
outgrowing baby things, the day when you stop
calling your mother. IHOP at midnight with
people who live in Instagram feeds and grass
between both pinky and teeth like the cigarette smoke
she makes love to in her garage (me, to the side). the turn
of a books last page and tap shoes
click-clacking on hospital floors, baby fat smiling
back at the wrinkles in the cotton bed, and the absence
of nightlights in coffins
(what if they're afraid
of the dark?).

Kyleigh Taylor

End Notes

i. My footnotes are footlings, notes are my noticing. Salamat datang. Sama sama, my sista, my brutha. 不客气 · 不谢. Woteva.

ii. The politics of language in Singapore is a fraught issue if you are, like me, a foreigner. The government says foreigners may have an agenda, or do not appreciate Asian ways culture. Fair enough. But I still have two cats there, Angelina and Mittens, so I feel I've a stake in the country. One has only half a tail and uses it as a fifth column when climbing trees.

iii. I explain all that "Lee Kuan Yew/poetry/cannot" stuff later.

iv. Inconveniently, considering how much I harp on about the Language Poets and that my essay is premised on Veronica Forrest-Thomson, I found little evidence directly linking her poetic theories to Marxism. Only the Marxist-informed voice of Roland Barthes screaming down the typed lines of dead-author history.

v. More inconvenience. The fact is Hamid Roslan, my central poet, may or not be directly influenced by Wittgenstein, the Language Poets, and Forrest-Thomson. Short of contacting him (which I did not want to do – what if, five days from the essay deadline, he tells me that he wasn't influenced?), I cannot find any reference to Forrest-Thomson in his work. Though there's the "forest" in the title of his book, parsetreeforestfire …

vi. Many Singaporeans are bilingual, as they are required to learn English and their "mother tongue", one of the other three official languages: Mandarin, Malay, or Tamil. I feel so inadequate.

vii. Roslan critiques Singapore's politics of language through form and context, showing how language has been co-opted by the state in the service of capitalism. Maybe I shouldn't say that, as it's hardly going to help him get an arts council grant.

viii. Joan Didion is not in this essay, but I want her to be.

ix. I wonder, who is "I"?

x. I am an outsider to South-East Asia, being a Westerner of European origin from New Zealand, although I lived in Singapore for some time. If my exploration seems reductive, I've avoided the complexity because the more I know, the more I realise my ignorance. That's not what you wanted to read, is it?

xi. I speak a version of English mangled by being a New Zealander and which was corrupted in the 1980s, when I worked on British tabloids. Weaning myself off speech punctuated by "Gotcha", I then lived in Singapore and so now my English incorporates elements of Singlish patois. Singlish colonised my English.

xii. Forrest-Thomson looks cool in her photos. Her hair is bobbed; reminds me of Katherine Mansfield.

xiii. Forrest-Thomson and Roslan were both born in South-East Asia – in the former's case, in 1947 in Penang. It may have only been one year of Forrest-Thomson's life in the tropics, but developmental studies have shown language acquisition begins in the womb. I suppose this is a bit tenuous.

xiv. I don't know Roslan at all, but once at a poetry reading he said nice things about my work.

xv. Maybe I should have ditched Forrest-Thomson and written an essay about "Echoes of Gertrude Stein in Hamid Roslan's Poetry"? Too late now.

xvi. Just because it is so beautiful, I am referencing Mary Oliver's West Wind, although it is from the Western canon and there are no echoes of it in Roslan's work.

Linda Collins

The Garden of Regret

First, you scour the garden for the perfect spot:
Where the sun hits, but clouds shield.
You tuck a rootless white seed into the earth; so pure, untainted.

Then, you wait and see, hope blossoms as a translucent petal; so faint, fragile. Sprouts. You water it with warm caresses and gentle kisses, watch in awe as it grows; big and mighty. Her branches rest atop the garden hedges as you tend to her stray leaves.

But you ignore the calling of the tree when she tells you to pluck,
Replying as you water the intertwined roots,
"They aren't in season yet."

Her leaves shed to shades of gold, this time she pleas. Please
Pick my apples.
You murmur in dismissal, voice drenched in the stench of fear,
"They are not ripe enough."

Alas, wind picks up, snow buries the Garden grounds. She does not beg this time. Hanging from her crooked branches, the lifeless corpses of brown apples. For you have missed when they were the finest of the land.

Liz Yew

My Soulmate

Your voice falls on me as they say love should,
Like an enormous yes
Our friendship became brotherhood.
Your voice falls on me as they say love should;
I was someone who you understood.
Who would guess
Your voice falls on me as they say love should
Like an enormous yes?

[Original quote: "On me your voice falls as they say love should, like an enormous yes" for Sidney Bechet by Phillip Larkin]

Max Wrigley

Garden of Regret

Regret is a common thing.
On unhealthy soil, it breeds rapidly.
Unconscious actions help the spiky plant to grow
with its stalk shooting up to prick your emotions unexpectedly.
Branches take a long time to form, which could feel like eternity
but when they do, they spawn healthy possibilities
that you might not have thought of, tempting resolution.
Harvest this cactus and you'll be on your way to solving problems
but miss the harvest and it will transform into a Venus fly trap,
which grips and swallows those that linger too long.

Max Wrigley

Come and find me, lying in the stream

Satsuma sun unpeels in molten sky.
Careful, don't get burned by all its juice-spray!
Now come and find me, lying in the stream,
Desiring all my love to wash away.

You stand above me on the muddy bank,
Your toes hugging the sudden steep decline.
But you can't find me lying in the stream.
You dread to hear the name I want as mine.

And pain's affixed upon your lovely face.
There's so much fear and hunger cast within
That even now you found me in the stream,
You'd let me drown before you would give in.

And I can't blame you, lying in the stream.
That's why I hid here in this lonely dell.
Though I confess those breadcrumbs all were mine,
I hoped you'd hear the ringing of my bell.

So though it makes sense when you turn your back,
And though I wryly smile instead of scream,
I do feel something fragile break apart
When you leave me lying in the stream.

Sammy Glyn

Psalm for the Drowning Sinner

This is not damnation; we would know it
      Were we damned,
The hot breath of the devil upon the nape
Of our necks.
We would beg for forgiveness,
      Yet, we here are not sinners,
And so we shall be saved.
We rejoice and sing, for we shall not be drowned.

In steady utterance we pray for those
Who shall be lost to the flood,
We will the retribution
      Of mothers grandmothers sinners atheists
For how could catastrophe lap at our ankles?
We rejoice, for we shall not be drowned.

Icy grip around our knees; freshwater
Minnows make their home in the narthex,
      Altar not yet submerged.
Candles battling against the black damp,
We rejoice, for we shall not be drowned.

The Vicar steadily ascending from the water,
Poised upon the pulpit, cassock sodden
And sending rivulets along the cracks of the stone.
He asking us to join hands and pray for those less
      Fortunate than ourselves.
And we rejoice, for we shall not be drowned.

I, under the current,
I, feeling my faith shake,
For god has abandoned me.
            Yet still, I rejoice; for I have not yet drowned.

Silas Hand

Judicial Review into Floodplain Management

In the face of rising water levels, the swelling banks of the river,
Perhaps we should've given more, planted
Witch Hazel and Viburnum as a gift to the current
So that when the houses became chimneys became nests for Herons
We could have said
> *yes, this is your land now, trace the pattern of your*
> *undercurrent and ecosystem Pond Skimmer and Stickleback*

Yet what we did say
> *just put your house on the market,*
> *some intrepid home renovator will*
> *drain the garden and replace it with a pool.*

There's plenty of land uphill where the lake doesn't grasp at your ankles
Plenty of land up the slope on the top amongst second homes
        and golf courses.
Plenty of land where the water isn't around your waist
Plenty of land and not riverbank

      Just keep faith it'll be over soon

Don't forget to vote for climate action in three years' time
      After which your address will be accessed by divers
As part of our judicial review into this tragedy.

Silas Hand

Growing pains

my growing pains aren't in my legs.
they're wrapped around the strands of my mother's graying hair,
held tightly between the ever-shrinking space
between my sister's head and mine,
they line the bricks of my childhood bedroom's walls.

my growing pains aren't buried down in my body.
they're in the walls of the school that held eleven year old me
between it's weather worn crumbling bricks,
in the press of the wind as I drive down that road
and can still see the ghost that is that little girl
barreling through the halls.
they're stretched taut across the branches
of the orchid tree in that playground
which has watched thousands of children
watch with still wide eyes
as it falls subject to time,
dancing in the leaves as they fall
so unaware and blissful.
I mourn this passing,
unheld hands stretching towards
threads that will only ever slip through my fingers,
there is nothing to grab.
the seasons will change anyway.

my growing pains aren't down in my bones.
but instead in the walls of a home I
technically can no longer call my own,
that has seen hate so strong it burns down bridges,
and love so full that it glows golden even when rotting.
they stretch between the pixels of old pictures,
immortalizing a time when youth allowed ignorance.
they're in the shake of my hand as I hug my best friend,
cradled by the curled syllables of

It's see you soon, not goodbye
pulled taut between the 106.4 miles that now carve between us,
living lives that were once indistinguishable
and are now
 - for the most part -
unfathomable.

my growing pains aren't in my side.
but held forever in the unreachable past of my life,
held in the moments that can only ever be viewed through memory now,
both nostalgic and nightmarish at once.
my growing pains are held in the hurt
that is the space between a yearning for the past
and the pull of the future,
the what if, and the what now
tugging tightly until your seams are ready to rip.
it's in always wanting the past and so missing the present,
an ouroboros of regret.
and i know all things change,
and nothing good lasts,
but does it have to go or leave or change so fast?

my growing pains aren't in my legs.
they're in the wish for a moment,
just one more,
that no amount of wishing will enable you to afford.
but if wishes are the currency of fools
then i'll spend my whole life being foolish.

Tallulah Cox

Poetry
Content Warning

Whatever Together

CW grief, death, illness

I have never asked if you liked your name.
Whenever I heard it I thought of you.
It doesn't have many letters or syllables, but it goes on a while
Like when you are waiting for someone to call you back or chasing moonlight.
That brief eternity.

You were talented at talking.
Whatever together with anyone and anybody.
You and I talked about a lot of things, together and apart.
I never dared to talk about the thought of outliving somebody.
One doesn't tend to think about the act of outliving
Because it is an act, you move towards it
Knowingly or unknowingly.
You don't want to admit that you know
That one day the sun will stop coming out.

You talked
Non-stop until the words
I want to go home.
Asking for your shoes
Until you stopped
Because a song has to stop somewhere.

Ellen Newall

Shh – Listen!

CW gore, gun violence, real world tragedies

1. The Corpse in the Mississippi

Authorities in the United States say a student opened fire at a high school north of Detroit, Michigan, killing three students and injuring eight other people, including a teacher.
-Aljazeera, Michigan School Shooting: Student kills three, injures eight, 30 Nov 2021.

I prefer the clamour in the silence to
The silence in the clamour. Just like
The splashing sound of the Mississippi
In the night, and
The chirping sound of the bird in
The gun shot.

That was the first encounter of me
And the boy who was around my age, with a gun
In his hand. When he said, you are arrested,
As if he was a policeman in the movie,
I heard the flapping sound of the wing of a pigeon
Flying through the window. And the next second,
He shot.
Like the sound of the door
Being slammed by someone rude.
And I don't know what happened next,
As I was packed into a gunny bag and thrown
Into the flowing rasping bleeding
Mississippi.

When the first sunlight
Lifts from the horizon, and burns the bleeding hole

Of my chest, I know
That my face has already turned
Wrinkled, like an old man
For soaking so long in the
Chilling water. But, my dear readers,
Bear in your mind: these are not wrinkles,
But a barcode of solitude, waiting
To be scanned.

2. A Dead Hiker of the Himalayas

Indian and Chinese soldiers were injured in another violent clash along the Himalayan border last week, as tensions between the two nuclear powers showed no signs of abating.
-The Guardian, Indian Troops Brawl with China Counterparts on Border, 25 Jan 2021

When the bullet struck
Into my temple, I can
Only hear the distant church bell
Ringing at three. Lunch time;
There were biscuits in my backpack, which I brought
For my hiking of the Himalayas
There was also a cup of hot
Americano – though it's been cold now,
I guess, whereas the cacophony of
The commanders of both sides, quarreling over who is responsible
For the skirmish, is still hot and burning
In my ears. My body, not far away
From them, is an invalid old coin which
No one will hanker and
Care.

Brandon Choo

'Opening'
CW themes of death

Another impossible orange;
it screams at me from lampposts
and gymnasiums. I want to unpeel it,
dislodge the dark, curled insect
from the amber and keep it, but colour
dunes upon its whitening skin
& collects beneath microscopic
mountain ranges, which shatter
as they scrape, into fragments
like a cranium.

I become the mad girl shaking
my dead geranium, tangerine petals
falling glamorously through a million
flickering changes, muscles in a human face
as it arranges and rearranges. We fall to bits
together, the thick woven ropes of religion
that anchor many others' ships
untethered. Like the dark waters
through which I move all steel and titanium
I disturb deep graves, thinking I'm a saviour.

The world is
no hospital though. Bones are heavy
with sleep, not hope; they sit
like blood in chambers,
a dead weight. Opening this fruit,
it's like draining rained land
of water, fitting a foot
into the print of a hand, or
the segments of a satsuma
back in the correct order.

I want to slot them into
my own crescent mouth,
to scaffold my smile without
upsiding down as
my lips press
and part
like mother and daughter;
press and
part, sea to coast;
dying into sleep & silence
on seperate pillows
to which they hold,
hold fast.
Like colour, lingering
where it's resented most.

E M Fawkes

Self-Talk

CW violence

What would you say, if you dodged through time's dance
With the knowledge of all you've lived through?
Which words would you choose, if you had the chance?
Not picked for past loved ones - but You.

If you had the chance to kneel at Your feet
And hold onto Your own tiny hands,
Would you pummel that child with your anger's full heat?
Or tell them they've ruined your plans?

The prospect's enough to make your heart crack.
Reminiscing eyes can easily blur.
In a reflection, those eyes looking back
Are just the same hue as Yours were.

So, do You a favour, and cut You some slack,
When talking to them in your mind.
They're trying so hard to keep things on track
So be kind, my friend, always be kind.

Esther Cornforth

locked doors

CW violence

I
see you
as a kind
of cabinet. Doors locked,
dark and dusty, you hide
away in shadows of yesterday's regret
and rise up in flames when the
rest of the world is asleep. The only
solace you know is the one you have created.
You thrive on reality that is distorted, warped, a broken
memory of the truth you experienced. There are padlocks on all
that you own, ivy that has strangled the walls in your garden
and the people who paint you blue and black, paint that runs red
on the darker days and drips onto the floor in a happy accident.
There
is no one you trust in the mirror, and you've looked inside yourself plenty of
times before. A surgeon brought to life; you search for parts that
refuse to function but
find they all seem to work somehow. Bruises line the mind not
the body. They remain invisible enough so that no one ever
seems to notice that you're locking the doors and pacing the
floors, slowly burying yourself into the ground, the ground you
seem to call home but it's not that at all and it never has been,
but you call it that anyway. It's a home tucked away, rearing off
the edge of a cliff as the waves thrash and threaten you from
down below. It's a minefield and you live there anyway. And
one day, perhaps it'll be less of a sinking ship and more a yacht
cruising on the coastline. But for now it's your home yet it's not a
home, but it's yours. And the locks, they aren't helping you at all,
they're keeping you afraid.

Eve Attwood

Thorns

CW gore, horror

He waited for you like a spider,
Window shopping for an easy target.
Eager hands hooked his toy,
Clean and fully loaded.

A boy of fifty years

Shrouded in withered skin
A finger pull from playing God,
You were struck and silenced.

Brambled arms cradled you above,
Concrete steeped in copper fluid
Spat from your body and gleamed off
Eyes like black plates.

Dreams never did seem so distant.

Helena Keys

thinking and other bad habits
CW depression

It's difficult being your own best friend
and simultaneously your own worst enemy; to love
being alone but feeling painfully lonely; to spend
days by yourself in your bedroom
and then weeks wanting nothing more than to escape your own
body and mind.
I have a detrimental habit of thinking.
No, overthinking.
Sometimes I even think about the fact I'm overthinking
and remind myself that I should stop overthinking
but I'm too busy thinking about overthinking to just stop thinking.

I get hopelessly lost in my thoughts;
my only wish
is that one day I stay
                                        lost;
wandering through the empty depths of my brain instead of
lying in my bed staring vacantly at the ceiling
when I should be in a class.

There are moments-
where I could be sitting in a classroom,
at a table in a coffee shop
or even in a loud bedroom at a friend's house-
in which I find myself dissecting things. Usually,
it's words. I picture a word in my head, as if it's printed on paper, and I begin to focus only on this word.

I repeat it to myself, silently and somewhat religiously,
over and over again until it no longer feels or looks like a word at

all.
Sometimes I even deconstruct myself too,
normally when I'm staring at my reflection in the mirror opposite my bed.
I often forget that although I've paused *my* life to pointlessly destroy the meaning of words,
the world around me is still marching on; full of pride and ignorance.

Time hasn't stopped to wait for me and neither have the people.

The people never seem to notice that I'm not there
but why would they?
I am right there.
I am sitting right next to them.
They could reach out and touch me.
But then again, I'm not there,
not really, not the me that matters anyway.
Not the me that laughs at their dark jokes or
sings along to the songs they play just because they know I love them-
only a shell of who I once was
and who I want to be remains with them.

Lily Gooch

The Dog is Dead
CW death

The dead dog came back
and now my body won't let me be loving.
My stomach lining is clear;
there is no air in my mother's car.

The dead dog came back
and now books look like the mouth of a pulpit
and music tugs like a baby's fist on an earring
and taking a shower is a total waste of my time.

The dead dog came back
and outside is barely full of chlorophyll,
grey, soft and dripping -
a wet dog on the doorstep.

I forgot to take my meds
so the dead dog came back
at the foot of my bed gnarled and groaning,
holding a pocket watch between his teeth
                              and counting.

Maya Elphick

Tat for tit

CW cancer, blood, hospitals

A breast reconstruction created
from my doughy belly.
A tummy tuck
- *two for the price of one!*

A stifling hospital room.

Relief when the Doppler ultrasound
finds a new pulse.

My daughter faints
at me
hooked up to four drains
of clotted blood worms.

A seroma leaking out
of my new belly button.

Later, silky scars snail
hip to hip,
axilla to axilla.

Dermal origami
creates a new nipple.
A new areola tattooed
with careful colour matching,
like mixing paint at Homebase.

A welcome prosthectomy.

Sarah Crowe

Prose

A Disturbance

At around 10:15 in the morning, Darren Jenkins was on his morning jog on the path that led out of the village, towards the hill that overlooked it. This went by the holiday home of the Crossley family, and on passing it he heard a loud crash. Pausing to check, he heard a second crash, and a third, and some loud bangs. Then there came a high-pitched shrieking, though he couldn't begin to think what it could come from.

He stopped at the gate that led to the driveway. It was closed and padlocked, and looking as far down the drive as he could, he didn't see any cars. Somebody was breaking into the Crossley's house. Just then, there came another one of those unearthly shrieks; he tried not to think about whether it was a somebody.

He abandoned his jog but made up for it by sprinting back to the village to call the police. All the way back, those shrieks continued. When he got to the police, he left out that aspect initially, focusing on the crashing sounds. The police contacted the Crossleys, who confirmed that they had left yesterday.

By this point, word had gotten out and had drawn the attention of the locals. Darren's village was one of those quiet country locales where a cat getting stuck up a tree was considered newsworthy. An actual crime happening was a once-in-a-lifetime event for many of the locals. Everyone was pestering Darren with questions about it, and before long he let it slip about the noises he heard.

This only added fuel to the rumours. There were all sorts of stories about the Crossleys, ever since they had arrived at that place; at least there were as of this morning. So, when Darren and the police went up to the house, the rest of the village tagged along.

By the time they reached the Crossley's house, the crashing and screaming had stopped. Peering through the windows, they could see shattered plant pots, smashed tables and chairs, and sofas with the stuffing pulled out. Then, on the wall of the dining room, where what seemed to be enormous scratch marks.

By now, even the policemen's hands were trembling as they turned the nearest doorknob. But it didn't budge. This door, and all the others, were locked.

Edward Grierson

'An inconvenient affair'

I remember meeting them at a party - it was summer and they were a friend of a friend. We were mutuals - 'were'. From our first 'hello', I heard the universe sigh. At our second rendezvous, I understood what the universe had meant - our timing was not in fate's cards. In less than five weeks, the journey of the rest of our lives began, and they were not planned to be together. As humans, we are told that love has no boundaries and that if it is meant to be, it will be. But what about 'right person-wrong time'? Surely there is no 'wrong time' with the right soul because if love has no boundaries, you can make it work? That sounds a little too optimistic to me.

We danced and we drank, simultaneously. I could tell that we both felt a sense of warmth within each other's presence. I learnt that we like to feed our souls with similar symphonies. And although this warmth and comfort evoked a blissful existence, I can't help but feel an angering intolerance. This new need of wanting to understand them deeply, wanting to grasp the things that speak to their soul is nothing short of intoxicating - because we aren't to be. We part our separate ways in less than a month before paving the way for the rest of our lives. 'I wish we met a year ago,' I said, 'at least we've met now' they say to me. Would I rather have not met them? If we hadn't crossed paths, I would not be feeling such animosity yet contentment.

Meeting you was a nice accident.

Hanna Rice-Smyth

HARPER

I make my way along the forest path. Moonlight streaks through the branches above me, and I realise that it would be such a nice night to be walking with a lover beside me.
Someone is following me, but I doubt they wish me well.
The creature hovers anxiously on the edge of my vision, little more than a pair of eyes peering from the hedgerows of raspberry bushes.
One of my hands is braced on the grainy wood of the gate, the other shakily retrieves a flask of tea from my backpack. The man who had almost drowned had given it to me in his drunken haze. I used some purple flowers to make tea - I hope it doesn't poison me, although death by tea wouldn't be the worst way to go.
Everything around me is dark, except the sky, which has faded from a flinty, moon-drunk grey.
The creature has made its way onto the path now – in the dark, it seems to be entirely made up of squirming black wool.
I've been standing here for about ten minutes now. Whenever I move, this creature moves with me.
I can handle most of the strange things in the woods – the badgers that scream and scuffle in the distance, the foxes that always stare like ghosts from the tops of rises, the rabbits that take off when I make a noise, their little white tails flashing like headlights as they vanish. I know there are more dangerous beasts out here - it's why I always close the gates. Even when there's no walls or fences on either side - those are the ones that the older folks always insist I close.
Out here, everything is in a limbo of life and death. There are old cars out here that have trees growing through them, but the cars look almost new, as if the trees burst from the ground and trapped them in place. Not far back, I'd seen a deer's rib cage lying propped in a tree trunk, now the framework of a bird's nest.
The creature has crept a little closer. We're now separated by the gate. I'd been told that gates had power.
I looked into its eyes, or whatever passed for eyes when it came to this.

This thing was old.
It had probably tricked half a dozen travellers into all sorts of wicked infernal deals. Its eyes screamed and raged in a language of folklore and anarchy.
Or maybe it was just a person. I could never be sure. Injecting ancient majesty into a stranger in the woods tended to make life a little more adventurous.
I offered it some tea.
A hand stretched out from the dark mass and took the flask. It held it for a moment, peering into the flask, then handed it back. The flask was considerably lighter. I didn't mind.
'Thank you,' it said. 'May your soul be overgrown with moss. May your veins fill with rainwater and your lungs with flowers. May you find your way back to the sea,'
It faded back into the hedgerows. I wonder if those words were a blessing, a curse, or a piece of abstract poetry, then I close the gate with a soft rattle.
I made my way home.
A little cottage in the middle of the woods. Light was glowing in the windows, and my cat was curled on the doorstep, staring keenly at me as I stepped up the path.
I went inside. My house was warmly lit – there's a fire burning in the grate, and a bathtub of goldfish and reeds sitting under the sink - all left over from a fair. They'd been difficult to carry home, but they made for better company then the cat, who liked to scratch. There's a row of shoes by the door. I added a worn pair of running shoes to the collection. A wood bowl of raspberries sits on the table.

Harper Day Pope

Albion

Grey were the waves, bashing and foaming against the lonely little boat. The girl sat at the front, praying for a horizon that was not another storm. Her father pulled in the tired oars, leant over the edge and threw up what little food the sea had given them. Her mother shivered, tears wetting her flushed cheeks as she cradled the screaming baby.

The girl took the oars and rowed, purple lightning flashing across the doomed sky. She took them further, thunder shaking the deathly high waves as if hell were trying to reach them. Then, far in the distance, a line appeared. It became clearer, boasting giant trees and vast stone beaches.

A bright smile shone from every part of the girl's face as if a shroud of midnight had been pulled away, revealing a rising sun.

'Land!' she cried out. 'Mother, Father, I see land!'

With her gaze fixed on the horizon, she rowed on, no wave being too high, her fingers red and sore from her grip on the oars. When they neared the beach, she jumped out of the boat, the icy water biting her bare feet. With her chapped and raw hands, she grabbed hold of the coarse rope and pulled their boat onto the rocky shore.

While her mother and father climbed out, the girl took the baby and calmed it. Then she gave it back to her mother, before grabbing her small satchel and leather flask from the boat.

Her father retched once more on the beach. Then he stood with his hand placed over his belly.

'The others did not make it,' he said.

'No,' said the girl, eyeing the forest past the beach. 'I think it's just us.'

They left their boat and the sea behind them. Pebbles scratched the girl's feet as she led her family towards the misty twist of trees. She took the first step through the forest, the singing of mysterious birds silencing the storm behind them. The ground felt soft beneath her feet, the dew-twinkling flowers gently tickling her toes. The sun broke through the forest's green canopy, and raindrops fell from the leaves and sparkled like dripping gold. The air was clear and perfect, as if born of the very first spring.

The girl walked ahead of her family. Then, she stopped and closed her eyes, finally, in the company of no one but herself. And though her lungs were free to breathe the purest of air, she was both curious and afraid of the thoughts that began to rise now that they had the freedom to do so.

In silence, the family carried on through the forest. By the time the sun rose to its highest point in the sky, the trees grew denser, as if their mossy trunks and drooping branches were made by a weaver woman.

'We must find food,' said her mother.

'No,' said the girl, before turning away. 'I want one more moment. Just one more for this land to be untouched.'

The girl tucked her long hair behind her ears then went ahead of her family. She found a narrow gap in the trees and squeezed through it. Then amongst brushing ferns, she came to a thick trunked tree, with broad branches, emerald leaves and long roots spreading across the ground like veins.

The girl carefully stepped over the roots, then she knelt before the tree. She raised her hand and gently rested her fingertips on the trunk, it both scratching and soothing, then she pressed her fingers and then her palm on it, until all that could be read on the lines of her hands was in the possession of the tree, telling it all that she was and all that she would ever be.

Then the girl whispered, 'Forgive us.'

Melissa Garrett

Gold Stars

Felix's second therapist is a nice lady in horn-rimmed glasses called Mette, who shakes his hand when he walks in and offers him a wrapped humbug from a bowl on her desk. Felix has never liked humbugs, but he takes one anyway to be polite; unwraps it, puts it in his mouth, traps it behind his teeth. Through it, he asks, "what does your name mean?"

He says it half to unnerve her: therapists get weird when you start asking them questions back. But if Mette is rattled, she doesn't let it show. "Pearl," she says, off-the-cuff like it's just something she knows. Felix is sort of unnerved back. "What about yours?"

"I don't know."

She smiles at him. "That can be your homework for next time." He finds that he likes Mette. His last therapist was a man who wore lots of patterned jumpers, who would always ask, "And how did that make you feel?" like he was trying to sort Felix into his assessment form, pressing him for answers that he could fit on a Likert Scale. Mette is the opposite: doesn't ever touch her pen, just sits and listens. She speaks like she has all the time in the world, savouring each word as though they're also humbugs in her mouth, which at the beginning he maybe finds a little annoying, but grows to appreciate. In his everyday life, which he sometimes feels like he lives at high speed, having a slow, deliberate weekly presence in his life, in the form of dusty candies and horn-rimmed glasses, is a cornerstone he comes to value.

Before he gets his final diagnosis, the doctors sort of hop around a variety of other disorders: ADHD, for a while, for which the medication fucking sucks, just makes him sluggish and irritable, and then depression, which is sort of half true, so the medication for that is a little better: settles his head, when he is in a dark recess. Does jackshit against the mania, though, until they finally fall on bipolar. It's during one of these recesses, his head still muddied a little, when Mette asks him how it feels.

"I don't know," he says. "Hard. Dark. I'm always tired." He turns his feet in together until the toes of his shoes meet under the frame of his chair. "Ironic."

"Why's that?"

"Do you wear that on purpose?" he says, of her necklace. It's a string of pearls.

Mette says, "Yes. But they're not real."

"Do you tell people that?"

"Of course not. I paid decent money for them to look real."

"You told me, though," he says.

"Why is it ironic, Felix?"

"Well. 'Cause I'm not happy, am I?" It's what his name means. He Googled it, after his first session: had laughed out loud when he saw the meaning. The universe sure has a good fucking sense of humour. Happy, for a boy who once spent five days without leaving his bed; it's also the word his mum used to use for his manic episodes before they knew they were manic episodes. "He's just happy!" she'd say, desperately, and then he slipped off the roof and broke his arm after thinking he could touch the sky. So yeah. He flicks the crucifix that hangs over their front door a middle finger whenever he leaves the house, now.

Later, as he is putting on his coat to leave, Mette says conversationally, "you know, I wear fake pearls because I'm allergic to real ones."

Felix pauses. "Really?"

"The universe is a strange fickle being that I don't pretend to understand," she says. She shrugs as if to emphasise. "But you wanted to know why I wear fake ones. That's why."

"So what are you saying? That I should just stick it to – what, the universe?"

"I'm saying find ways around it. How does it feel? After the worst?"

"Like I have to learn to be happy again."

The next time, with the customary humbug, Mette hands him a sheet of stickers.

"What's this?" he says.

"Teach yourself to be happy."

It's a pack of forty-nine gold stars, seven by seven, the paper slippery in his hand. He doesn't really know what to do with them, so he carefully folds the sheet, careful not to bend any of the stars, and tucks it into his pocket. "Thanks," he says, but doesn't really mean it. He thinks she's still making him pay for how he entered the first session: there's always something out-of-pocket. Last session it was a big spider brooch he'd tried not to spend the entire hour staring at.

"Bring them the next session," she says. "You can talk to me about the ones you've used."

He doesn't get it until he walks out of her office, and it starts to rain. He's wearing a hooded sweatshirt and it's not a far walk to the bus stop, but it's still annoying, so he squares his shoulders, folds himself deeper into his hoodie, and puts his hands in his pockets.

Then, from down the road, he sees two people exit a store, halfway through lighting cigarettes. They step into the rain and the girl says, "Shit!" and they quickly flick off the lighter, bending down to keep the cigarettes dry and huddle underneath the awning. The boy says something and the girl starts to laugh, and Felix pauses, watching as the boy takes both of their unlit cigarettes, puts them into his pocket, and pulls her into a kiss.

By the time Felix walks past the shop, they've disappeared into the alley. He reaches into his pocket, pulls out the sheet of stickers, and presses a small gold star to the wall where they stood.

Mia Galanti

morning, the bathroom, home.

Stately, plump, shaving foam across the jaw. Foaming - line thin as a hair shaved in, straighter than hair but hairline. Neighbour all these years, and never once aware of each other. Why did he move his mirror? Light's better there, I suppose. Get the tricky corners of the jaw. Time is it? Always, and not yet. Awfully tired. Anaemic maybe? Or not. Just tired. Every day, though; that can't be normal, and then everyone is, all the time. Half a beard now, over there. Two different faces.

    He used to shave his right jaw first, every morning. All those years. Don't suppose he knew he was doing it that way. Unconscious habit. Wonder what mine are although that's their unconsciousness. Right jaw, left jaw, chin. None of this Gillette razor nonsense. Cut-throat. Could. But didn't, of course. Might as well have done for all the good not doing it did. 46 years old. No time for the earth. Two decades of daily mundanity but this time here in the sweet dent of old lady skull.

    Maudlin. Beardless man. Shouldn't watch a fellow in his bathroom. Naughty. Unless he doesn't know, which he doesn't, and it isn't out of meanness. Just a crazy old lady, flattened opposite, squared into window boxes, fishtank menagerie of human. Not my fault metropolitan life is so compact. Sticks of butter in the shape of people. People probably watch me wrap towels around for 28 years. Different people before then. 60 years of neighbourly towel swaddles. Nothing private. Not anymore. Francis spits white mint against white porcelain, swills it out and dilutes it down the drain. She pulls her own face towards her until it disappears over her shoulder. The cabinet is a mess. Pill bottles without order, half-punctured Paracetamol packets, pierced foil in little tiny piles beside it.

    Not a good week.

    Solid chemicals. Chemical ice cube. Packed in together, boxed up, prescribed, and taken. Work when they work and otherwise they don't. Much. Life is. Take this: you'll be happy. Take it: pain stop. Take it: pain doesn't stop but pain tries to stop. Otherwise, work it out yourself. Might as well have done for all the good it didn't.

    Mirror assembled back against the wall. Man in it, in his window in his house, in her mirror, man beardless and smooth. Man brushing his own teeth. How old? 20s? No. 30s. Never was good at numbers. Stan? No, younger. Younger for sure, but not by much. Girlfriend? Could not assume. Eyes will be kept out.

    Handful of water, wash the happy down. Happy happy. Another. Wash the muscle-soother down. 20s, 30s, none of this nonsense. Oh dear. To be young. To be brim-full of uncertain, uncertain even of what you're uncertain; if only they would swap it around and replace it with questions. Questions do have answers, don't they? They will know that one day. Too late then, of course, that's the way of things.

    Cup of tea. Only thing for it. Time? Yes. Half an hour. Time for tea, so time for tea.

    Last visited, when? Before the lockdown, that's certain. Oh dear. Memory is a fragile thing. Is that new though?

    December. Beginning of. Nora with the stories of little paper doors - day 8 she said it was.
8 little chocolates, Nanna!
8? My, my you are a lucky thing!
My love. My delight.
Yes which means there's…
Little fingers employed. Thoughtful. 24-8. Equals.
Means there's… 15 more chocolates before
16, Dear.
16, yes, 16 more chocolates before the big day. Mum says that's okay though because then I might get more from… Do you believe in Father Christmas, Nana?
Of course, dear. How could I not?
Oh good so you're not one of the boring adults. Stephen said that Santa wasn't…

Stephen. No sense of delight. Must live vicariously through them, we must. Too young to realise that, too old to do it. He'll come round. Pedantic age, that. Shame. Realise it and it's too late. All the good it does.

    Leaf drink. Restorative leaf drink. Make a pot, perhaps? Pot for Patrick, and Molly. Nora - hot chocolate? In the cupboard? No. Not. Substituted. Never can count on a substitution - Horlicks instead. Would she like Horlicks? No. Old man drink. Squash for Nora. Unless I send Stephen when they get here. Will ask. Always worth asking.

    Limescale.

    Knock knock.

    Early? Very early? Not like them, not at all.

Molly Phillips

His Green Heart.

I once had a friend. Their heart was green.
Friend, I call them, for I know not what they were.
I met them at the yule ball. I in the corner, scanning the dimly lit room: the dancing, the feasting, the joyous song. But it was not for me, an orphan, a peasant's child. Not a kind glance in sight.
Red. His lips. His smile. I saw it through the crowd, by the great doors, brighter than the dusty torches that surrounded it. Flickering unfaithfully. I could hardly see through the crowd. But I could still see him. Those bright white eyes. His green heart.
They were looking at me.
I could feel it. I had nothing else. I had to move to them. Throwing myself through the dancers, clambering under tables. I had to get to him.
He led me with his red, his white, that warm green heart, leaking into mine.
Then I was outside. The storm still raging on the cliffs. I could see naught but him. He was at the tree. That old, gnarled oak, its hard black bark now quivered in the wind, its roots dangling. Winter's grasp threatened to pull it over. Down into the sea.
I made my way to him. The sight of his red lips warmed me. His white eyes fell around me, they were in the air, they engulfed the land. The wind howled around us, nothing else was there. I made my way to him. I needed that smile. I could not lose it.
Then I reached him. Standing by the tree. A writhing mass of green dressed the bare tree. His eyes, his smile. They formed patterns on the tree. Red berry lips and white berry eyes. The green heart. The tree and him. They both grinned.
I kissed him, felt his breath. Red flew down my throat. Burned inside me. Warm. Pulsating. Skin in the snow. White stained with red and…black. The tree's black bark, its arms in long tendrils wrapped round us. Kept us warm. My lone friend and I, together in the snow, forging angels. The white of our frostbitten skin, the white of the snow. I am one with the cold and warmth. Wanted.
Then we were in the tree. Felt it rumble. But that Heart, green

and throbbing. It moved out of him, it stretched out. It moved into me. It was not his Heart. The red, the white. His whole had been consumed. He was not his own. Perhaps he never had been.
That heart. Too green. The heart wanted too much, too much that it could not have. It would claim me.
But then I saw it. In my mind, my mothers pale smile, her kind eyes as she faded with me in her arms. It was not like his smile. Not like his eyes. There was no love. Not in that heart. But somewhere further…perhaps I saw a tear. And yet I could not reach it.
This was not what I wanted. Not what I needed. So, I broke free. Ran naked through the snow. Found warmth in the hall. And warmth is all I need.
I wish my friend could know this warmth.
I shed a tear for his fate.
A tear for his green heart.

Oli Hurley

The Merman

I saw the Merman for the last time one Thursday evening. He was where I had left him, beached again on the bank, snoring. The sun warmed the stones on the beach, and dappled my bag and trousers as it shone through the willow leaves above. I sat down on the concrete steps and pulled a beer as quietly as I could, not wanting to wake him. The smell of fish was faint, claggy and sweet in the warmth. I opened the beer with care, but the sound roused him. He rolled over and, seeing me, began calling.

"Ahoy! Ahoy boy, ahoy!"

I pulled another, and sent it down the bank towards him. Lunging, he caught it and popped the tab off. It burst out all over his chin and chest. "Like finest sea foam, straight from the mouth of Triton!" he said. It was a Stella.

I sipped at my own, and watched him. He had his beer nestled on his belly, and weeds in his hair. He was bloating. When a fish bloats and balloons to the surface, eyes bugged out and mouth swollen open, it fills water with death. I tipped the rest of my beer back, and chucked another down for the Merman. He grinned as he caught it.

"Did I ever tell you of the Aegean." It wasn't a question, so I didn't say anything.

"Great shoals of fish! Gorgeous, gorgeous fish. Beautiful, with the light all shining off them from the sun. You could sneak a hand in and just pluck one out with your hand, break its neck and drink the flesh, it was so tender!" He squished the rest of the beer can into his mouth, licked his chops and ripped the top off the next, grinning all the while at me.

"One time, I came across a great field of clams. A veritable bounty! O, the sea was kind to me that day! And they were rare too, only grew around that bit of coast, they were so rare. Hadn't seen them in years."

He wriggled, and I caught a whiff.

"And what did you do with those clams, oh Merman."

"Why, ate them of course! Ate every single one. And you know what?"

I sipped my beer. I wondered what he could be about to say. "Best meal I ever had." He threw back his head and laughed at the sky, rolling on the gravel, thrashing stones off into the undergrowth with his tail. I saw it then, the wound in his side. There was something in there, something infecting the flesh. I could see the white meat becoming brown, the edges, pink masses throbbing and clotting. He must have seen me looking, because he stopped laughing suddenly and rolled over on his side, hiding it under his blubber.

"Give me another beer, give me another."

"You haven't finished yours." I took a sip.

"I told you a tale, didn't I?"

"Tell me another."

He snarled at me, bared his greenish teeth. I pulled an old fishhook from the brush next to me, and threw it down at him. He flinched.

"Why are you here in the Thames? Why don't you go back to the Aegean?" I stood, holding the beer out in front of me as I stepped closer.

The merman watched me with a sneer upon his blue lips. He was shivering. In the warmth of summer his skin was cracked. He trembled.

"Show me the wound in your side." I demanded. "Show me."

The beer can glittered, as I stepped into the sunlight.

He rolled over. Through the top of his tail a black harpoon had pierced. It had torn the scales as it entered, and now they hung as rags. The flesh was blackened and dripping, sloughed down his side like a line of pitch. There was poison there. There was poison deep inside that wound, I smelt it in the air and saw it in the clouding of his swelling, pained eyes.

"Pull it out?"

"'Tis barbed."

I looked at the handle, it was splintering. Dropping the beer, I stepped forth and grasped it in both hands, as the Merman roared.

"Let me drive it through then, let me help!"

The Merman's voice lapped up and down in pain as spittle caulked his lips.

"Leave me be!"

I gripped the cold of the barb, braving the stink as pus swelled up from the harpoon.

"You lie here on the bank of the Thames, rotting, telling tall tales and snatching beer cans. What kind of creature are you?"

"Leave me be, damn you!"

I let go of the harpoon, and he pushed himself away from me.

"How did you get it? Who did this?"

The Merman pushed himself up on his elbows, shuddering in pain as he made himself comfortable, leaning his weight off his wound. I went to the river, and washed the muck from my palms. The Merman took the last can of Stella, drank deeply, and closed his eyes. The final rays of the sun came down and lit the river in gold. Warmth began to leak from the summer evening as it became night. I could still smell the rot as I climbed the steps, and went off down the footpath.

Sam Kirk

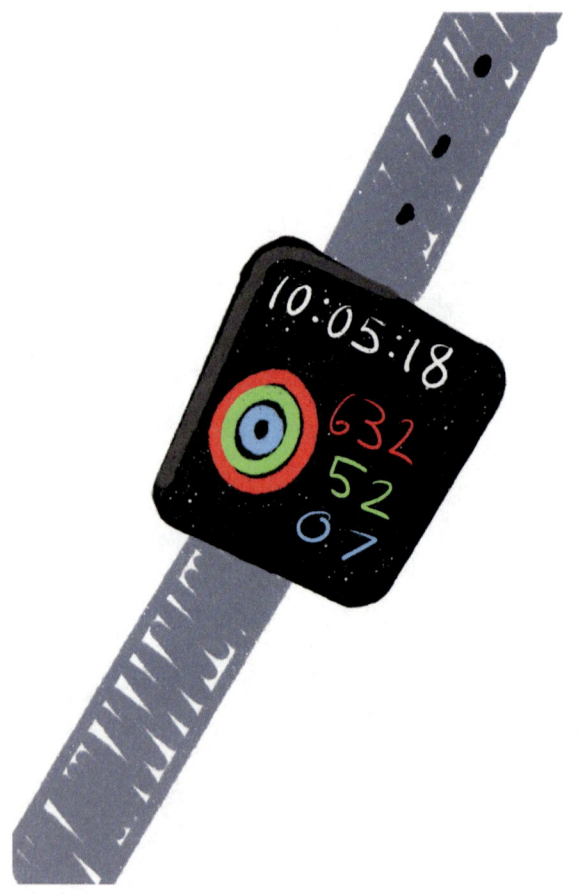

Prose

Content Warning

Before
CW death

In the moments before my death, I did not dwell on that time I overslept, the grades and jobs I didn't get and the time I wasted.

In the moments before my death, I thought of the lake. I thought of the ducks that swam across it. Families? Packs? I can't quite think of the collective noun for ducks. But they were together and I was alone but I wasn't full of jealousy but admiration. I could see the ducklings following their mother like shrunken shadows and I smiled wondering how a world of such dysfunction could be home to a sight so pure and delicate. During moments like these, I liked to close my eyes and focus on the sound of my own heart. A young heart. The beat rippled from my chest to my hand that was upon it. It was a metronome for me alone and I treasured that. Breathing was effortless yet purposeful, with every inhale I brought my fatigued body to life. Moments of serenity are sacred. I know this now.

A quickening of steps and a breathlessness disturbed me and I was met with a friendly face that looked as if it desired nothing more than to become my acquaintance. A fluffy face and a tag named "Lily". How nice it must be to be so unaware? I'm not sure if ignorance truly is bliss but it's hard to deny it when seeing a face as happy as yours.

I thought of my old student house, the mouldy ceiling and the broken drawers. I wondered if those walls kept our memories, I should've pencilled "Eleanor was here" in the dark corners. I remembered when we all moved in and I saw the transformation of a dreary, overpriced, worn-down house into a home. The live laugh love sign was the centrepiece, I'm sure my housemate curses me for that to this day. I want to sit on the step by the back door once more and smoke a final cigarette, adding to the pile of butts on the floor like pebbles on a beach. Drunken evenings and dazed mornings spent here, where party clothes would turn into dressing gowns. Times where I would exhale polluted breath into polluted air. I didn't have to worry about my crackled skin or aching joints then, what would break would surely fix.

In the moments before my death, I thought of the bus journeys where I would put on my headphones and escape the world for 40 minutes. Looking back felt like a stereotypical scene from a coming-of-age movie that I believed myself to be the main character of, so absorbed in myself and the universe in my mind. Sometimes, I would type in my notes app on my phone, on low brightness to shield my words from spectators, as if they even cared for jumbled thoughts translated into pixels. These times were write-offs, necessary wasted time for journey but I enjoyed every moment. Obviously, this didn't include the school buses where kids and their hefty backpacks swarmed. This was after tipsy nights, library visits or simply just times in the city with my friends. The upstairs of the double-decker was empty besides myself and a few other souls with books, headphones or some just gazing out the window. The silence was never awkward.

In the moments before my death I did not think of the misery and plagued thoughts. I simply smiled and fell away.

Eleanor Lewis

Lifeblood

CW distressing images, fire

Dalli turned from the flaming corridor, sweat and burns upon her. A voice called to her, piercing the smoke and death.

"Run, Dalli, now! Over here!"

The neon lights of the skyscraping city. The thrum of a ship's flight engine. A hand outstretched, gloved and saving.

Red. Black. Blades. Jolts. Lightning swerving across her vision.

Dalli looked about her, the ground swaying like waves beneath her. The very air crumbled to ash, the sky shattering into dying shards; the earth shuddered, as it perished.

There was screaming, she was certain of it.

Dalli listened. Someone crying, a woman. Wailing, grief-stricken and terrified.

Dalli realised it was her.

Nighttime. Daytime. Starlight. Sun. All blurred together, forming a drowsy veil above her. The morbid carpet of reality.

Dalli fell to the floor, jaw bleeding salt, wounds leaking spice. Her fingers turned to stone, and her eyes became rubies upon a crown.

Someone stood over her: a man. His feet were stone too, his fingers of the deepest obsidian, his chest of the richest gold.

The wind lifted her up, turned her over, made her look, helped her see.

"Dalli, thank goodness. Are you alright?"

His eyes were emerald. And amethyst. But this man wore no crown. His head was a grave, a monument to the dead.

In that grave she saw her name.

"Dalli, talk to me! What happened here?"

And his.

Gulls cawed above a rocking shore. Old men frolicked beneath an alabaster cliff. Travellers fell at the foot of the pyramid. Life. Joy. Grief. Death. All were the same. All were limbs on the body of reality.

Dalli stared at the pit. A million bodies waited in the depth, a million dimensions of light and matter, a million singularities of meshing geometry and clashing dashing gnashing paradox.

The pit smiled a question. Dalli smiled an answer.

Was this what it was to be real? To be saved?

She took a step. Her foot fell, and its echo lasted an age. She took another. This one sounded for instants. Then her hands, raised and ready, went forth, and peeled back the face of fabric reality.

Dash. Three. Delta. Eight. Two. Two. Dot. Four. Four. Dash. Omega. Nine. Slash.

The code of the worlds. The code of the dimensions. The lifeblood of life itself.

Dalli saw the heart of the Earth, pulsing and dead to the heart of men.

Her fingers traced over the digits and dials of reality, editing and skimming and cutting and trimming and copying and printing and pasting the essence of atomic existence.

"Hey! We've got company incoming! Do you have it yet?"

Time rolled like a marble, cast by the hand of fate, the hand of those in power. But where was it rolling, and why would it never begin? Or was it always beginning, and so it never ended?

Light. Red. Black. Stone. Grave. Shores. Pyramids. Bodies. Numbers. Blood. Marble.

Darkness.

Dalli saw darkness now.

Dalli saw darkness.

She saw

She

He

Kryze outstretched his hand, eyes alit with fear, as the chamber crumbled about them. Dalli simply stood before him, pupils glazed, skin bleached with absence. Her lips were singed at the edges.

"Dalli, please. Come back. I need you. I can't do this without you."

He

She

She saw

Darkness abandoned, light reborn.

Dalli saw him. Dalli knew him.

And Dalli would save him.

Evan Denison

Juliet
CW sex

It was a week before uni let out for summer holidays, and I'd failed an exercise in class again. The drama teacher had instructed us to practise crying on cue, and I'd tried, I really had, but when it was my turn to burst into tears, I couldn't. The teacher offered a condescending, pitiful smirk and the other students stifled laughter. It wasn't a rare occurrence. I was a bad actress, but I was determined to play Juliet, someday. I went to the sort of arts uni where you could turn up to a seminar in full body camo and a helmet and call it War-Core. You could get away with shit. You could get away with being a bad actress. But it was my third year, and the fact that I still couldn't cry made me feel hopelessly small.

Whenever I felt the weight of the world was crushing me, I'd walk to Danny's on my lunch hour. Danny was three years older than I was. He had hair the colour of straw which he wore in a mullet that looked like it had been cut with hedge trimmers. His eyes were the colour of icy pond water. He was rail-thin and often visibly hungover. Danny had been my elder brother's best friend through A-levels. During that year I'd developed a friendship with him that centred mainly around him slipping me sips of Strongbow under the table at barbecues and once biting the soft flesh of my ear at a school disco before glimpsing my peaky face under a flash of strobe light, pushing me away and muttering, Jesus Christ, sorry, I forget you're still a foetus.

He had a job that involved a lot of phone calls and emailing. He worked from home and didn't get out of bed until noon, and when I went round to his bedsit in Herne Hill, I often had to knock until my hand was sore. But when I arrived that particular day in June, he was sitting on the steps. Rolling cigarettes on his knee, a bony jut covered in faded beige corduroy. He was not very dexterous at that hour of the day. Amber Leaf was scattered like confetti. A Bluetooth speaker playing SoundCloud grime reverberated at his elbow.

You don't often get to see people being born, and you don't often get to see them dying. But you see them smoking every day. Life holding Death in its hands. In goes Death, out goes Life, soft little curls of grey on the wind. I said this out loud and Danny laughed. He didn't laugh with sound. His mouth opened, his head tilted back, and his eyes scrunched up and he shook. If I had been watching a silent film, I'd have thought he was weeping, hysterically.

He said, Well, you know, Juliet, 100% of non-smokers die. He rolled a cigarette, put it in his mouth, lit it, and passed it to me. I blew smoke in his face and asked when he planned to start calling me by my real name again. When you stop obsessing over playing Juliet, he said. I'll call you by your real name when you quit trying to be someone else.

I'm an actress. Being someone else is what I do.

Fuck that. Get a proper job.

I won't quit till I play Juliet. And I can't play Juliet till I can cry on cue.

Look at the career you've chosen. You're already just like Juliet, Ophelia, Desdemona... An absolute sucker for pain and emotional torment. Think on that and let the tears come, little masochist.

Jesus, that's a pretentious thing to say.

He shrugged. I'm not saying you shouldn't keep trying. I didn't really like your name, anyway. You'll need money, though, and you won't get that from acting.

I flicked ash at him and said, Speaking of filthy lucre, last week, this Texan exchange student in my theatre class asked me if Herne Hill was anything like Notting Hill. Both being Hills, I guess that was the connotation.

Danny laughed soundlessly: For fuck's sake. Americans, dumber than shite. Fancy an ice cream? Milky Bar. Iceland, reduced. He went inside to retrieve the ice creams. He returned, shucking the wrappers away, and handed me one. We sat in the sun and licked at them idly.

After a few minutes, the silence bored me. I had a short attention span that summer, so I told him an anecdote about my boyfriend. I told Danny how, after the last time we had had sex, he was buckling his pants, and said to me, wrinkling his nose, that I smelled like cum. I'd said Well, obviously I smell like cum, I'm sure Mummy didn't tell you that the white stuff was salad cream. Or did she?

Danny laughed and swore: Jesus. Break up with him already.

Danny liked to tell people to stop doing things; stop dating your boyfriend, stop attending drama school, stop rooming with girls who still dye their hair with Manic Panic and listen to MCR. If I had stopped doing everything he told me to, I would have had nothing to do but sit on the steps with him and smoke. In retrospect, I think that's what he wanted, but he didn't say it out loud, and I didn't figure it out until it was too late. I only understood it years later, when Danny and his rented room in Herne Hill were only a brief moment in the vortex of memories from the year that I was 20 and callous and longing to be Juliet.

The funny thing is, it's like turning on a tap, now. Whenever I'm on stage, I think of that afternoon smoking cigarettes on the steps, and I cry. Afterwards, everyone says, how do you do it? How do you make it seem so real? I say, because it is real. Acting isn't lying; it's telling the truth.

I wish I'd known that sooner.

Ingrid Jensen

Oblivion

CW murder, bereavement

Today is Saturday. My alarm would have gone off at seven-thirty in the morning, with the sound of an impatient trailer honking on a busy freeway. Chuchu, my little sister, would have heard it and turned on her side but would refuse to be roused. Our mother would have marched into our room minutes later, to draw open the curtains and sprinkle cold water on anyone still found in bed. On any other Saturday, all these would have taken place in my house, but no, not today.

Gbola, my boyfriend, would have sent me at least three text messages, arranging our usual Saturday rendezvous of partying around town. He would have arrived at about noon, parked down the road, after Mama Philo's house, and then, flashed my phone to let me know that he was around. Then, I would have left the house on the pretext of going to the salon, with my hair wrapped tightly in my favourite black scarf. Holding a black bag bearing my party outfit for the day... a bag I would have hidden outside the house earlier, to prevent stirring my father's suspicions, I'd saunter over to his car. My usual Saturday rituals would have been waived today, since nothing's usual about this Saturday.

My Instagram page would have been agog with activity today. With two parties on my itinerary, pictures and videos would have flooded my timeline. My Twitter handle would have kept up with every trend of the day, earning me likes, follows, tweets and shares. If today had been a typical Saturday, my followers would have grown on both accounts by at least another hundred or more. But typical is one thing today is not, so none of these would have happened on social media.

Yet, today is a special day all the same. My name is on the lips of one and all, as everyone tries to find out where I am... what has happened to me. I can see all that they are doing and know all that they didn't do. I see myself as well, floating on the Lagoon

where those pesky brigands dumped me, after robbing our bus yesterday morning. Discontented with taking my money, my pearl costume earrings and my palasa phone, they hacked me all over and threw me out of the bus, leaving the remaining passengers stunned.
Everything that would have happened today no longer matters… at least, to me they don't.

Temi Taiwo-Oni

Defy the Devil

CW Holocaust mention

War. Total annihilation. The possible extinction of all that we know and love, of every memory, of all that makes life precious, of everything that says I existed.   And yet, the drumbeat, the lust for blood, the desire to hurt, to relieve our own pain continues to this day. Only when the mirrored, soulless, and compassionless eyes of the Grim Reaper make us realise our one true fear- the fear of vanishing without a trace of ourselves left behind- do we realise, only too late, that there is no war to end all wars.

A city, once proud and imperial in its majesty, and now a place of suffering, misery, and hatred. A place that was united in its beauty is now a place divided by ugliness.

Two opposing commanders with their fingers on the red button that will destroy what is before you had a chance to see what could be. It begs the question, who will be brave enough, or angry enough, to do the right thing?

Both commanders stare out over the ruins of what was once home. It is hard to believe that this was once a paragon of history, culture, and civility and that now it is a graveyard without dignity or remembrance. The smells and sights of death are so overwhelming that even the Sun seems to have abandoned its sacred duty. It is even harder to believe that both commanders were once human beings, with hopes and dreams, fears, and vulnerabilities, even childhoods, just as we have. Whether there will be a tomorrow and people to see it is in the hands of these two men.

They continue to stare each other down with righteous condemnation from their ivory, but very real, towers on opposite sides. The red buttons, so reminiscent of the buttons that, as children, they both used to launch toy rockets, glow with a hellish delight at the thought of so many condemned souls. As if the hypnotic lure of the buttons has been broken, both commanders suddenly notice the outside world, and each other, as if for the first time. Not as enemies of law and order, or menaces to society, but as fellow human beings. Naturally, one commander hears the words spoken by those who deny the rights and hopes of us all, that malevolent yet reasonable voice that manipulates destruction wherever it goes, and where one hears it, so does another.

"You know, don't you, that if you let compassion weaken you, your enemy will not hesitate to destroy you."

"Why are you hesitating? An enemy of order deserves no mercy!"

The lines have been chiselled into minds with surgical precision, yet so has the quality of mercy. Killing a fellow person would be like killing ourselves, and it is that that prevents the selfish machinations of some from destroying the many.

Both commanders survey the place below that they both once called home, and it occurs to them how although the threat of extinction looms over them, the people they claim to speak for are trying to regain some sense of normality in their lives. The family whose home was bombed having to move in with their neighbours. A woman with a baby trying to keep it warm and safe. A butcher whose shop was destroyed, now selling meat in the streets. Perhaps for the first time, the commanders have seen the people that they adamantly claim to fight for as people who have their own battles to fight, people who are just trying to make it through to tomorrow, people who cling to the smallest sliver of happiness in a world that has been deprived of it.

The realisation strikes them with the crescendo of a clock striking midnight. Hundreds, thousands, millions…perhaps more, of people, who have no idea that their lives could be erased with the touch of a button, whose fates are now in the hands of two people who claim to be right. It is this moment, more than any other, that gives hope for the future. The first commander allows himself to question an idea that became the truth, and as they press their face against the distorted window, a tear slowly

rolls down his face. As if sensing weakness from their enemy, the second commander smiles with devilish glee, only to see the people they swore to keep alive at any cost, in a strangely ironic twist, making peace with their anger and hatred in the hope that tomorrow will be better than today. The second commander, now caught up in the emotions once denounced as weak and obsolete, looks at the button, and then up at their enemy.
Both commanders are now in conflict; their hatred tells them that the other is the enemy and needs to be destroyed; yet the human soul, buried and thought forgotten, reminds them that to wipe one out is to wipe out themselves. The red button no longer looks like a toy. To press it will not launch a toy rocket, but a real weapon. A weapon that has been used before, to devastating effect, and it was hoped that it would never be used again. The city, once home and paradise to all who wanted nothing more than a new life, lies in ruins, a symbol of humanity's refusal to learn from the Holocaust, from Hiroshima and Nagasaki, from the times that unleashed an unholy monster that almost destroyed what good we had left. It is a refuge more than a home, as whoever is left has nowhere else to go. If destruction remains the only answer, then it will not matter anymore. This is a nightmare. It is not prophecy; indeed, it is the desperate prayer of all people of good conscience that it need never be. But it does happen.

There is no moral, only fact. All that can be said is this… are both commanders still human, and will we as an extension of them rediscover our humanity in time?

William Mckinnel

FIN

Becca Blake

The University of East Anglia's Creative Writing Society

Committee 2021-2022

President:	Clara Ehlers
Vice-President:	Ellen Newall
Secretary:	Barnaby Hill
Treasurer:	Sammy Glyn
Social Secretary:	Mackenzie Malcolm
Health & Safety Officer:	Silas Hand
Equality & Diversity Officer:	Biff Pearson
First Year Representative:	Evan Denison

With special thanks to Nathan Hamilton & Oliver Hancock with the UEA Publishing Project.
Cover design by Becca Blake.
Typesetting by Mackenzie Malcolm.
Interior illustrations by Mackenzie Malcolm.